THINGS OF THIS WORLD

Also by Richard Wilbur

THE BEAUTIFUL CHANGES and Other Poems

CEREMONY and Other Poems

Molière's THE MISANTHROPE (Translator)

A BESTIARY (Editor)

Things of This World

Poems by Richard Wilbur

Harcourt, Brace and Company, New York

The poems "Boy at the Window," "The Beacon,"
"Exeunt" (originally published under the title "Ex-
odus"), 1952; "Merlin Enthralled," "After the Last
Bulletins," "A Black November Turkey," 1953; "All
These Birds," 1955; copyrighted in the respective years
shown by The New Yorker Magazine, Inc.

"Beasts," "A Prayer to Go to Paradise with the Don-
keys," and "The Pelican" appeared in *A Bestiary*, by
Richard Wilbur, copyright, 1955, by Pantheon Books,
Inc.

C.5.57

Other poems have appeared in *Audience, Beloit
Poetry Journal, Botteghe Oscure, Furioso, Harvard
Advocate, Hudson Review, Imagi, Inventario, Ken-
yon Review, Mandrake, Nimbus, Origin, Paris Re-
view, Partisan Review, Poetry,* Trinity College
Review, Spectrum, and *Wake.*

LIBRARY OF CONGRESS CATALOG CARD NUMBER: 56-6655

PRINTED IN THE UNITED STATES OF AMERICA

For
ELLEN,
CHRISTOPHER,
and
NATHAN

CONTENTS

THINGS OF THIS WORLD

ALTITUDES

I

Look up into the dome:
It is a great salon, a brilliant place,
    Yet not too splendid for the race
Whom we imagine there, wholly at home

    With the gold-rosetted white
Wainscot, the oval windows, and the fault-
    Less figures of the painted vault.
Strolling, conversing in that precious light,

    They chat no doubt of love,
The pleasant burden of their courtesy
    Borne down at times to you and me
Where, in this dark, we stand and gaze above.

    For all they cannot share,
All that the world cannot in fact afford,
    Their lofty premises are floored
With the massed voices of continual prayer.

II

    How far it is from here
To Emily Dickinson's father's house in America;
    Think of her climbing a spiral stair
Up to the little cupola with its clear

    Small panes, its room for one.
Like the dark house below, so full of eyes
    In mirrors and of shut-in flies,
This chamber furnished only with the sun

Is she and she alone,
A mood to which she rises, in which she sees
   Bird-choristers in all the trees
And a wild shining of the pure unknown

   On Amherst. This is caught
In the dormers of a neighbor, who, no doubt,
   Will before long be coming out
To pace about his garden, lost in thought.

LOVE CALLS US TO THE THINGS
OF THIS WORLD

The eyes open to a cry of pulleys,
And spirited from sleep, the astounded soul
Hangs for a moment bodiless and simple
As false dawn.
                  Outside the open window
The morning air is all awash with angels.

    Some are in bed-sheets, some are in blouses,
Some are in smocks: but truly there they are.
Now they are rising together in calm swells
Of halcyon feeling, filling whatever they wear
With the deep joy of their impersonal breathing;

    Now they are flying in place, conveying
The terrible speed of their omnipresence, moving
And staying like white water; and now of a sudden
They swoon down into so rapt a quiet
That nobody seems to be there.
                      The soul shrinks

    From all that it is about to remember,
From the punctual rape of every blessèd day,
And cries,
             "Oh, let there be nothing on earth but laundry,
Nothing but rosy hands in the rising steam
And clear dances done in the sight of heaven."

    Yet, as the sun acknowledges
With a warm look the world's hunks and colors,
The soul descends once more in bitter love
To accept the waking body, saying now
In a changed voice as the man yawns and rises,

"Bring them down from their ruddy gallows;
Let there be clean linen for the backs of thieves;
Let lovers go fresh and sweet to be undone,
And the heaviest nuns walk in a pure floating
Of dark habits,
                    keeping their difficult balance.'

SONNET

The winter deepening, the hay all in,
The barn fat with cattle, the apple-crop
Conveyed to market or the fragrant bin,
He thinks the time has come to make a stop,

And sinks half-grudging in his firelit seat,
Though with his heavy body's full consent,
In what would be the posture of defeat,
But for that look of rigorous content.

Outside, the night dives down like one great crow
Against his cast-off clothing where it stands
Up to the knees in miles of hustled snow,

Flapping and jumping like a kind of fire,
And floating skyward its abandoned hands
In gestures of invincible desire.

PIAZZA DI SPAGNA,
EARLY MORNING

I can't forget
How she stood at the top of that long marble stair
Amazed, and then with a sleepy pirouette
Went dancing slowly down to the fountain-quieted square;

Nothing upon her face
But some impersonal loneliness,—not then a girl,
But as it were a reverie of the place,
A called-for falling glide and whirl;

As when a leaf, petal, or thin chip
Is drawn to the falls of a pool and, circling a moment above it,
Rides on over the lip—
Perfectly beautiful, perfectly ignorant of it.

JOHN CHRYSOSTOM

He who had gone a beast
Down on his knees and hands
Remembering lust and murder
Felt now a gust of grace,
Lifted his burnished face
From the psalter of the sands
And found his thoughts in order
And cleared his throat at last.

What they heard was a voice
That spoke what they could learn
From any gelded priest,
Yet rang like a great choir,
He having taught hell's fire
A singing way to burn,
And borrowed of some dumb beast
The wildness to rejoice.

A BLACK NOVEMBER TURKEY

to A. M. *and* A. M.

Nine white chickens come
With haunchy walk and heads
Jabbing among the chips, the chaff, the stones
    And the cornhusk-shreds,

And bit by bit infringe
A pond of dusty light,
Spectral in shadow until they bobbingly one
    By one ignite.

Neither pale nor bright,
The turkey-cock parades
Through radiant squalors, darkly auspicious as
    The ace of spades,

Himself his own cortège
And puffed with the pomp of death,
Rehearsing over and over with strangled râle
    His latest breath.

The vast black body floats
Above the crossing knees
As a cloud over thrashed branches, a calm ship
    Over choppy seas,

Shuddering its fan and feathers
In fine soft clashes
With the cold sound that the wind makes, fondling
    Paper-ashes.

The pale-blue bony head
Set on its shepherd's-crook
Like a saint's death-mask, turns a vague, superb
And timeless look

Upon these clocking hens
And the cocks that one by one,
Dawn after mortal dawn, with vulgar joy
Acclaim the sun.

MIND

Mind in its purest play is like some bat
That beats about in caverns all alone,
Contriving by a kind of senseless wit
Not to conclude against a wall of stone.

It has no need to falter or explore;
Darkly it knows what obstacles are there,
And so may weave and flitter, dip and soar
In perfect courses through the blackest air.

And has this simile a like perfection?
The mind is like a bat. Precisely. Save
That in the very happiest intellection
A graceful error may correct the cave.

AFTER THE LAST BULLETINS

After the last bulletins the windows darken
And the whole city founders readily and deep,
Sliding on all its pillows
To the thronged Atlantis of personal sleep,

And the wind rises. The wind rises and bowls
The day's litter of news in the alleys. Trash
Tears itself on the railings,
Soars and falls with a soft crash,

Tumbles and soars again. Unruly flights
Scamper the park, and taking a statue for dead
Strike at the positive eyes,
Batter and flap the stolid head

And scratch the noble name. In empty lots
Our journals spiral in a fierce noyade
Of all we thought to think,
Or caught in corners cramp and wad

And twist our words. And some from gutters flail
Their tatters at the tired patrolman's feet,
Like all that fisted snow
That cried beside his long retreat

Damn you! damn you! to the emperor's horse's heels.
Oh none too soon through the air white and dry
Will the clear announcer's voice
Beat like a dove, and you and I

From the heart's anarch and responsible town
Return by subway-mouth to life again,
Bearing the morning papers,
And cross the park where saintlike men,

White and absorbed, with stick and bag remove
The litter of the night, and footsteps rouse
With confident morning sound
The songbirds in the public boughs.

LAMARCK ELABORATED

"The environment creates the organ"

The Greeks were wrong who said our eyes have rays;
Not from these sockets or these sparkling poles
Comes the illumination of our days.
It was the sun that bored these two blue holes.

It was the song of doves begot the ear
And not the ear that first conceived of sound:
That organ bloomed in vibrant atmosphere,
As music conjured Ilium from the ground.

The yielding water, the repugnant stone,
The poisoned berry and the flaring rose
Attired in sense the tactless finger-bone
And set the taste-buds and inspired the nose.

Out of our vivid ambiance came unsought
All sense but that most formidably dim.
The shell of balance rolls in seas of thought.
It was the mind that taught the head to swim.

Newtonian numbers set to cosmic lyres
Whelmed us in whirling worlds we could not know,
And by the imagined floods of our desires
The voice of Sirens gave us vertigo.

Though the unseen may vanish, though insight fails
And doubter and downcast saint
Join in the same complaint,
What holy things were ever frightened off
By a fly's buzz, or itches, or a cough?
Harder than nails

They are, more warmly constant than the sun,
At whose continual sign
The dimly prompted vine
Upbraids itself to a green excellence.
What evening, when the slow and forced expense
Of sweat is done,

Does not the dark come flooding the straight furrow
Or filling the well-made bowl?
What night will not the whole
Sky with its clear studs and steady spheres
Turn on a sound chimney? It is seventeen years
Come tomorrow

That Bruna Sandoval has kept the church
Of San Ysidro, sweeping
And scrubbing the aisles, keeping
The candlesticks and the plaster faces bright,
And seen no visions but the thing done right
From the clay porch

To the white altar. For love and in all weathers
This is what she has done.
Sometimes the early sun
Shines as she flings the scrubwater out, with a crash
Of grimy rainbows, and the stained suds flash
Like angel-feathers.

MERLIN ENTHRALLED

In a while they rose and went out aimlessly riding,
Leaving their drained cups on the table round.
Merlin, Merlin, their hearts cried, where are you hiding?
In all the world was no unnatural sound.

Mystery watched them riding glade by glade;
They saw it darkle from under leafy brows;
But leaves were all its voice, and squirrels made
An alien fracas in the ancient boughs.

Once by a lake-edge something made them stop.
Yet what they found was the thumping of a frog,
Bugs skating on the shut water-top,
Some hairlike algae bleaching on a log.

Gawen thought for a moment that he heard
A whitethorn breathe *Niniane*. That Siren's daughter
Rose in a fort of dreams and spoke the word
Sleep, her voice like dark diving water;

And Merlin slept, who had imagined her
Of water-sounds and the deep unsoundable swell
A creature to bewitch a sorcerer,
And lay there now within her towering spell.

Slowly the shapes of searching men and horses
Escaped him as he dreamt on that high bed:
History died; he gathered in its forces;
The mists of time condensed in the still head

Until his mind, as clear as mountain water,
Went raveling toward the deep transparent dream

Who bade him sleep. And then the Siren's daughter
Received him as the sea receives a stream.

Fate would be fated; dreams desire to sleep.
This the forsaken will not understand.
Arthur upon the road began to weep
And said to Gawen *Remember when this hand*

Once haled a sword from stone; now no less strong
It cannot dream of such a thing to do.
Their mail grew quainter as they clopped along.
The sky became a still and woven blue.

A VOICE FROM UNDER THE TABLE
to Robert and Jane Brooks

How shall the wine be drunk, or the woman known?
I take this world for better or for worse,
But seeing rose carafes conceive the sun
My thirst conceives a fierier universe:
And then I toast the birds in the burning trees
That chant their holy lucid drunkenness;
I swallowed all the phosphorus of the seas
Before I fell into this low distress.

You upright people all remember how
Love drove you first to the woods, and there you heard
The loose-mouthed wind complaining *Thou* and *Thou;*
My gawky limbs were shuddered by the word.
Most of it since was nothing but charades
To spell that hankering out and make an end,
But the softest hands against my shoulder-blades
Only increased the crying of the wind.

For this the goddess rose from the midland sea
And stood above the famous wine-dark wave,
To ease our drouth with clearer mystery
And be a South to all our flights of love.
And down by the selfsame water I have seen
A blazing girl with skin like polished stone
Splashing until a far-out breast of green
Arose and with a rose contagion shone.

"A myrtle-shoot in hand, she danced; her hair
Cast on her back and shoulders a moving shade."
Was it some hovering light that showed her fair?
Was it of chafing dark that light was made?

Perhaps it was Archilochus' fantasy,
Or that his saying sublimed the thing he said.
All true enough; and true as well that she
Was beautiful, and danced, and is now dead.

Helen was no such high discarnate thought
As men in dry symposia pursue,
But was as bitterly fugitive, not to be caught
By what men's arms in love or fight could do.
Groan in your cell; rape Troy with sword and flame;
The end of thirst exceeds experience.
A devil told me it was all the same
Whether to fail by spirit or by sense.

God keep me a damned fool, nor charitably
Receive me into his shapely resignations.
I am a sort of martyr, as you see,
A horizontal monument to patience.
The calves of waitresses parade about
My helpless head upon this sodden floor.
Well, I am down again, but not yet out.
O sweet frustrations, I shall be back for more.

THE BEACON

Founded on rock and facing the night-fouled sea
A beacon blinks at its own brilliance,
Over and over with cutlass gaze
Solving the Gordian waters,

Making the sea-roads out, and the lounge of the weedy
Meadows, finding the blown hair
As it always has, and the buxom, lavish
Romp of the ocean-daughters.

Then in the flashes of darkness it is all gone,
The flung arms and the hips, meads
And meridians, all; and the dark of the eye
Dives for the black pearl

Of the sea-in-itself. Watching the blinded waves
Compounding their eclipse, we hear their
Booms, rumors and guttural sucks
Warn of the pitchy whirl

At the mind's end. All of the sense of the sea
Is veiled as voices nearly heard
In morning sleep; nor shall we wake
At the sea's heart. Rail

At the deaf unbeatable sea, my soul, and weep
Your Alexandrine tears, but look:
The beacon-blaze unsheathing turns
The face of darkness pale

And now with one grand chop gives clearance to
Our human visions, which assume

The waves again, fresh and the same.
Let us suppose that we

See most of darkness by our plainest light.
It is the Nereid's kick endears
The tossing spray; a sighted ship
Assembles all the sea.

STATUES

These children playing at statues fill
The gardens with their shrillness; in a planned
And planted grove they fling from the swinger's hand
Across the giddy grass and then hold still

In gargoyle attitudes,—as if
All definition were outrageous. Then
They melt in giggles and begin again.
Above their heads the maples with a stiff

Compliance entertain the air
In abrupt gusts, losing the look of trees
In rushed and cloudy metamorphoses,
Their shadows all a brilliant disrepair,

A wash of dodging stars, through which
The children weave and then again undo
Their fickle zodiacs. It is a view
Lively as Ovid's Chaos, and its rich

Uncertainty compels the crowd:
Two nuns regard it with habitual love,
Moving along a path as mountains move
Or seem to move when traversed by a cloud;

The soldier breaks his iron pace;
Linked lovers pause to gaze; and every rôle
Relents,—until the feet begin to stroll
Or stride again. But settled in disgrace

Upon his bench, one aging bum,
Brought by his long evasion and distress
Into an adamantine shapelessness,
Stares at the image of his kingdom come.

Five soldiers fixed by Mathew Brady's eye
Stand in a land subdued beyond belief.
Belief might lend them life again. I try
Like orphaned Hamlet working up his grief

To see my spellbound fathers in these men
Who, breathless in their amber atmosphere,
Show but the postures men affected then
And the hermit faces of a finished year.

The guns and gear and all are strange until
Beyond the tents I glimpse a file of trees
Verging a road that struggles up a hill.
They're sycamores.   The long-abated breeze

Flares in those boughs I know, and hauls the sound
Of guns and a great forest in distress.
Fathers, I know my cause, and we are bound
Beyond that hill to fight at Wilderness.

II. But trick your eyes with Birnam Wood, or think
How fire-cast shadows of the bankside trees
Rode on the back of Simois to sink
In the wide waters. Reflect how history's

Changes are like the sea's, which mauls and mulls
Its salvage of the world in shifty waves,
Shrouding in evergreen the oldest hulls
And yielding views of its confounded graves

To the new moon, the sun, or any eye
That in its shallow shoreward version sees

24

The pebbles charging with a deathless cry
And carageen memorials of trees.

III. Now, old man of the sea,
    I start to understand:
    The will will find no stillness
    Back in a stilled land.

    The dead give no command
    And shall not find their voice
    Till they be mustered by
    Some present fatal choice.

    Let me now rejoice
    In all impostures, take
    The shape of lion or leopard,
    Boar, or watery snake,

    Or like the comber break,
    Yet in the end stand fast
    And by some fervent fraud
    Father the waiting past,

    Resembling at the last
    The self-established tree
    That draws all waters toward
    Its live formality.

Charles Baudelaire: L'INVITATION AU VOYAGE

My child, my sister,
dream
How sweet all things would seem
Were we in that kind land to live together,
And there love slow and long,
There love and die among
Those scenes that image you, that sumptuous weather.
Drowned suns that glimmer there
Through cloud-disheveled air
Move me with such a mystery as appears
Within those other skies
Of your treacherous eyes
When I behold them shining through their tears.

There, there is nothing else but grace and measure,
Richness, quietness, and pleasure.

Furniture that wears
The lustre of the years
Softly would glow within our glowing chamber,
Flowers of rarest bloom
Proffering their perfume
Mixed with the vague fragrances of amber;
Gold ceilings would there be,
Mirrors deep as the sea,
The walls all in an Eastern splendor hung—
Nothing but should address
The soul's loneliness,
Speaking her sweet and secret native tongue.

There, there is nothing else but grace and measure,
Richness, quietness, and pleasure.

See, sheltered from the swells
There in the still canals
Those drowsy ships that dream of sailing forth;
It is to satisfy
Your least desire, they ply
Hither through all the waters of the earth.
The sun at close of day
Clothes the fields of hay,
Then the canals, at last the town entire
In hyacinth and gold:
Slowly the land is rolled
Sleepward under a sea of gentle fire.

There, there is nothing else but grace and measure,
Richness, quietness, and pleasure.

DIGGING FOR CHINA

"Far enough down is China," somebody said.
"Dig deep enough and you might see the sky
As clear as at the bottom of a well.
Except it would be real—a different sky.
Then you could burrow down until you came
To China! Oh, it's nothing like New Jersey.
There's people, trees, and houses, and all that,
But much, much different. Nothing looks the same."

I went and got the trowel out of the shed
And sweated like a coolie all that morning,
Digging a hole beside the lilac-bush,
Down on my hands and knees. It was a sort
Of praying, I suspect. I watched my hand
Dig deep and darker, and I tried and tried
To dream a place where nothing was the same.
The trowel never did break through to blue.

Before the dream could weary of itself
My eyes were tired of looking into darkness,
My sunbaked head of hanging down a hole.
I stood up in a place I had forgotten,
Blinking and staggering while the earth went round
And showed me silver barns, the fields dozing
In palls of brightness, patens growing and gone
In the tides of leaves, and the whole sky china blue.
Until I got my balance back again
All that I saw was China, China, China.

Francis Jammes: A PRAYER TO GO TO
PARADISE WITH THE
DONKEYS

to Máire and Jack

When I must come to you, O my God, I pray
It be some dusty-roaded holiday,
And even as in my travels here below,
I beg to choose by what road I shall go
To Paradise, where the clear stars shine by day.
I'll take my walking-stick and go my way,
And to my friends the donkeys I shall say,
"I am Francis Jammes, and I'm going to Paradise,
For there is no hell in the land of the loving God."
And I'll say to them: "Come, sweet friends of the blue skies,
Poor creatures who with a flap of the ears or a nod
Of the head shake off the buffets, the bees, the flies . . ."

Let me come with these donkeys, Lord, into your land,
These beasts who bow their heads so gently, and stand
With their small feet joined together in a fashion
Utterly gentle, asking your compassion.
I shall arrive, followed by their thousands of ears,
Followed by those with baskets at their flanks,
By those who lug the carts of mountebanks
Or loads of feather-dusters and kitchen-wares,
By those with humps of battered water-cans,
By bottle-shaped she-asses who halt and stumble,
By those tricked out in little pantaloons
To cover their wet, blue galls where flies assemble
In whirling swarms, making a drunken hum.
Dear God, let it be with these donkeys that I come,
And let it be that angels lead us in peace
To leafy streams where cherries tremble in air,

29

Sleek as the laughing flesh of girls; and there
In that haven of souls let it be that, leaning above
Your divine waters, I shall resemble these donkeys,
Whose humble and sweet poverty will appear
Clear in the clearness of your eternal love.

Philippe de Thaun: THE PELICAN

PELLICANUS is the word
    For a certain breed of bird
Who truly is a crane;
    Egypt is his domain.
There are two kinds thereof;
    Near to the Nile they live;
One of them dwells in the flood,
    The fishes are his food;
The other lives in the isles
    On lizards, crocodiles,
Serpents, and stinking creatures,
    And beasts of evil nature.
In Greek his title was
    Onocrotalos,
Which is *longum rostrum,* said
    In the Latin tongue instead,
Or *long-beak* in our own.
    Of this bird it is known
That when he comes to his young,
    They being grown and strong,
And does them kindly things,
    And covers them with his wings,
The little birds begin
    Fiercely to peck at him;
They tear at him and try
    To blind their father's eye.
He falls upon them then
    And slays them with great pain,
Then goes away for a spell,
    Leaving them where they fell.
On the third day he returns,
    And thereupon he mourns,

31

Feeling so strong a woe
   To see the small birds so
That he strikes his breast with his beak
   Until the blood shall leak.
And when the coursing blood
   Spatters his lifeless brood,
Such virtue does it have
   That once again they live.

K N O W that this pelican
   Signifies Mary's Son;
The little birds are men
   Restored to life again
From death, by that dear blood
   Shed for us by our God.
Now learn one meaning more,
   Revealed by holy lore:
Know why the small birds try
   To peck their father's eye,
Who turns on them in wrath
   And puts them all to death.
Men who deny the light
   Would blind God's blazing sight,
But on such people all
   His punishment will fall.
This is the meaning I find;
   Now bear it well in mind.

APOLOGY

A word sticks in the wind's throat;
A wind-launch drifts in the swells of rye;
Sometimes, in broad silence,
The hanging apples distil their darkness.

You, in a green dress, calling, and with brown hair,
Who come by the field-path now, whose name I say
Softly, forgive me love if also I call you
Wind's word, apple-heart, haven of grasses.

Paul Valéry: H E L E N

It is I, O Azure, come from the caves below
To hear the waves clamber the loudening shores,
And see those barks again in the dawn's glow
Borne out of darkness, swept by golden oars.

My solitary hands call back the lords
Whose salty beards beguiled my finger-tips;
I wept. They sang the prowess of their swords
And what great bays fled sternward of their ships.

I hear the martial trumpets and the deep-
Sea conches cry a cadence to the sweeps;
The oarsmen's chantey holds the storm in sway;

And high on the hero prows the Gods I see,
Their antique smiles insulted by the spray,
Reaching their carved, indulgent arms to me.

BEASTS

Beasts in their major freedom
Slumber in peace tonight. The gull on his ledge
Dreams in the guts of himself the moon-plucked waves below,
And the sunfish leans on a stone, slept
By the lyric water,

In which the spotless feet
Of deer make dulcet splashes, and to which
The ripped mouse, safe in the owl's talon, cries
Concordance. Here there is no such harm
And no such darkness

As the selfsame moon observes
Where, warped in window-glass, it sponsors now
The werewolf's painful change. Turning his head away
On the sweaty bolster, he tries to remember
The mood of manhood,

But lies at last, as always,
Letting it happen, the fierce fur soft to his face,
Hearing with sharper ears the wind's exciting minors,
The leaves' panic, and the degradation
Of the heavy streams.

Meantime, at high windows
Far from thicket and pad-fall, suitors of excellence
Sigh and turn from their work to construe again the painful
Beauty of heaven, the lucid moon
And the risen hunter,

Making such dreams for men
As told will break their hearts as always, bringing
Monsters into the city, crows on the public statues,
Navies fed to the fish in the dark
Unbridled waters.

EXEUNT

Piecemeal the summer dies;
At the field's edge a daisy lives alone;
A last shawl of burning lies
On a gray field-stone.

All cries are thin and terse;
The field has droned the summer's final **mass;**
A cricket like a dwindled hearse
Crawls from the dry grass.

MARGINALIA

Things concentrate at the edges; the pond-surface
Is bourne to fish and man and it is spread
In textile scum and damask light, on which
The lily-pads are set; and there are also
    Inlaid ruddy twigs, becalmed pine-leaves,
    Air-baubles, and the chain mail of froth.

Descending into sleep (as when the night-lift
Falls past a brilliant floor), we glimpse a sublime
Décor and hear, perhaps, a complete music,
But this evades us, as in the night meadows
    The crickets' million roundsong dies away
    From all advances, rising in every distance.

Our riches are centrifugal; men compose
Daily, unwittingly, their final dreams,
And those are our own voices whose remote
Consummate chorus rides on the whirlpool's rim,
    Past which we flog our sails, toward which we drift,
    Plying our trades, in hopes of a good drowning.

BOY AT THE WINDOW

Seeing the snowman standing all alone
In dusk and cold is more than he can bear.
The small boy weeps to hear the wind prepare
A night of gnashings and enormous moan.
His tearful sight can hardly reach to where
The pale-faced figure with bitumen eyes
Returns him such a god-forsaken stare
As outcast Adam gave to Paradise.

The man of snow is, nonetheless, content,
Having no wish to go inside and die.
Still, he is moved to see the youngster cry.
Though frozen water is his element,
He melts enough to drop from one soft eye
A trickle of the purest rain, a tear
For the child at the bright pane surrounded by
Such warmth, such light, such love, and so much fear.

SPEECH FOR THE REPEAL OF THE McCARRAN ACT

As Wulfstan said on another occasion,
The strong net bellies in the wind and the spider rides it out;
But history, that sure blunderer,
Ruins the unkempt web, however silver.

I am not speaking of rose windows
Shattered by bomb-shock; the leads touselled; the glass-grains
    broadcast;
If the rose be living at all
A gay gravel shall be pollen of churches.

Nor do I mean railway networks.
Torn-up tracks are no great trouble. As Wulfstan said,
It is oathbreach, faithbreach, lovebreach
Bring the invaders into the estuaries.

Shall one man drive before him ten
Unstrung from sea to sea? Let thought be free. I speak
Of the spirit's weaving, the neural
Web, the self-true mind, the trusty reflex.

ALL THESE BIRDS

Agreed that all these birds,
Hawk or heavenly lark or heard-of nightingale,
Perform upon the kitestrings of our sight
In a false distance, that the day and night
Are full of wingèd words
                    gone rather stale,
        That nothing is so worn
        As Philomel's bosom-thorn,

        That it is, in fact, the male
Nightingale which sings, and that all these creatures wear
Invisible armor such as Hébert beheld
His water-ousel through, as, wrapped or shelled
In a clear bellying veil
                    or bubble of air,
        It bucked the flood to feed
        At the stream-bottom. Agreed

        That the sky is a vast claire
In which the gull, despite appearances, is not
Less claustral than the oyster in its beak
And dives like nothing human; that we seek
Vainly to know the heron
                    (but can plot
        What angle of the light
        Provokes its northern flight.)

        Let them be polyglot
And wordless then, those boughs that spoke with **Solomon**
In Hebrew canticles, and made him wise;
And let a clear and bitter wind arise

To storm into the hotbeds
                        of the sun,
      And there, beyond a doubt,
      Batter the Phoenix out.

      Let us, with glass or gun,
Watch (from our clever blinds) the monsters of the sky
      Dwindle to habit, habitat, and song,
      And tell the imagination it is wrong
      Till, lest it be undone,
                        it spin a lie
         So fresh, so pure, so rare
         As to possess the air.

      Why should it be more shy
Than chimney-nesting storks, or sparrows on a wall?
      Oh, let it climb wherever it can cling
      Like some great trumpet-vine, a natural thing
      To which all birds that fly
                        come natural.
         Come, stranger, sister, dove:
         Put on the reins of love.

A BAROQUE WALL-FOUNTAIN
IN THE VILLA SCIARRA

for Dore and Adja

Under the bronze crown
Too big for the head of the stone cherub whose feet
   A serpent has begun to eat,
Sweet water brims a cockle and braids down

   Past spattered mosses, breaks
On the tipped edge of a second shell, and fills
   The massive third below. It spills
In threads then from the scalloped rim, and makes

   A scrim or summery tent
For a faun-ménage and their familiar goose.
   Happy in all that ragged, loose
Collapse of water, its effortless descent

   And flatteries of spray,
The stocky god upholds the shell with ease,
   Watching, about his shaggy knees,
The goatish innocence of his babes at play;

   His fauness all the while
Leans forward, slightly, into a clambering mesh
   Of water-lights, her sparkling flesh
In a saecular ecstasy, her blinded smile

   Bent on the sand floor
Of the trefoil pool, where ripple-shadows come
   And go in swift reticulum,
More addling to the eye than wine, and more

Interminable to thought
Than pleasure's calculus. Yet since this all
  Is pleasure, flash, and waterfall,
Must it not be too simple? Are we not

  More intricately expressed
In the plain fountains that Maderna set
  Before St. Peter's—the main jet
Struggling aloft until it seems at rest

  In the act of rising, until
The very wish of water is reversed,
  That heaviness borne up to burst
In a clear, high, cavorting head, to fill

  With blaze, and then in gauze
Delays, in a gnatlike shimmering, in a fine
  Illumined version of itself, decline,
And patter on the stones its own applause?

  If that is what men are
Or should be, if those water-saints display
  The pattern of our areté,*
What of these showered fauns in their bizarre,

  Spangled, and plunging house?
They are at rest in fulness of desire
  For what is given, they do not tire
Of the smart of the sun, the pleasant water-douse

  And riddled pool below,
Reproving our disgust and our ennui

    * Note: *areté*, a Greek word meaning roughly "virtue."

44

With humble insatiety.
Francis, perhaps, who lay in sister snow

    Before the wealthy gate
Freezing and praising, might have seen in this
    No trifle, but a shade of bliss—
That land of tolerable flowers, that state

    As near and far as grass
Where eyes become the sunlight, and the hand
    Is worthy of water: the dreamt land
Toward which all hungers leap, all pleasures pass.

AN EVENT

As if a cast of grain leapt back to the hand,
A landscapeful of small black birds, intent
On the far south, convene at some command
At once in the middle of the air, at once are gone
With headlong and unanimous consent
From the pale trees and fields they settled on.

What is an individual thing? They roll
Like a drunken fingerprint across the sky!
Or so I give their image to my soul
Until, as if refusing to be caught
In any singular vision of my eye
Or in the nets and cages of my thought,

They tower up, shatter, and madden space
With their divergences, are each alone
Swallowed from sight, and leave me in this place
Shaping these images to make them stay:
Meanwhile, in some formation of their own,
They fly me still, and steal my thoughts away.

Delighted with myself and with the birds,
I set them down and give them leave to be.
It is by words and the defeat of words,
Down sudden vistas of the vain attempt,
That for a flying moment one may see
By what cross-purposes the world is dreamt.

A CHRONIC CONDITION

Berkeley did not foresee such misty weather,
Nor centuries of light
Intend so dim a day. Swaddled together
In separateness, the trees
Persist or not beyond the gray-white
Palings of the air. Gone
Are whatever wings bothered the lighted leaves
When leaves there were. Are all
The sparrows fallen? I can hardly hear
My memory of those bees
Which only lately mesmerized the lawn.
Now, something, blaze! A fear
Swaddles me now that Hylas' tree will fall
Where no eye lights and grieves,
Will fall to nothing and without a sound.

I sway and lean above the vanished ground.

THE MILL

The spoiling daylight inched along the bar-top,
Orange and cloudy, slowly igniting lint,
And then that glow was gone, and still your voice,
Serene with failure and with the ease of dying,
Rose from the shades that more and more became you.
Turning among its images, your mind
Produced the names of streets, the exact look
Of lilacs, 1903, in Cincinnati,
—Random, as if your testament were made,
The round sums all bestowed, and now you spent
Your pocket change, so as to be rid of it.
Or was it that you half-hoped to surprise
Your dead life's sound and sovereign anecdote?
What I remember best is the wrecked mill
You stumbled on in Tennessee; or was it
Somewhere down in Brazil? It slips my mind
Already. But there it was in a still valley
Far from the towns. No road or path came near it.
If there had been a clearing now it was gone,
And all you found amidst the choke of green
Was three walls standing, hurdled by great vines
And thatched by height on height of hushing leaves.
But still the mill-wheel turned! its crazy buckets
Creaking and lumbering out of the clogged race
And sounding, as you said, as if you'd found
Time all alone and talking to himself
In his eternal rattle.
                              How should I guess
Where they are gone to, now that you are gone,
Those fading streets and those most fragile lilacs,
Those fragmentary views, those times of day?
All that I can be sure of is the mill-wheel.
It turns and turns in my mind, over and over.

FOR THE NEW RAILWAY STATION
IN ROME

Those who said God is praised
By hurt pillars, who loved to see our brazen lust
　　Lie down in rubble, and our vaunting arches
　　　　Conduce to dust;

Those who with short shadows
Poked through the stubbled forum pondering on decline,
　　And would not take the sun standing at noon
　　　　For a good sign;

Those pilgrims of defeat
Who brought their injured wills as to a soldiers' home;
　　Dig them all up now, tell them there's something new
　　　　To see in Rome.

See, from the travertine
Face of the office block, the roof of the booking-hall
　　Sails out into the air beside the ruined
　　　　Servian Wall,

Echoing in its light
And cantilevered swoop of reinforced concrete
　　The broken profile of these stones, defeating
　　　　That defeat

And straying the strummed mind,
By such a sudden chord as raised the town of Troy,
　　To where the least shard of the world sings out
　　　　In stubborn joy,

"What city is eternal
But that which prints itself within the groping head

49

Out of the blue unbroken reveries
Of the building dead?

"What is our praise or pride
But to imagine excellence, and try to make it?
What does it say over the door of Heaven
But *homo fecit?*"